MAKING CHRIST KNOWN

A Decade Handbook

Philip King

Illustrations by 'Taffy'

CHURCH HOUSE PUBLISHING
Church House, Great Smith Street, London SW1P3NZ

ISBN 0 7151 5531 8

Published 1992 for the General Synod Board of Mission
by Church House Publishing

© *The Central Board of Finance of the Church of England 1992*

All rights reserved. No part of this publication may be reproduced or stored or transmitted by any means or in any form, electronic or mechanical, including photocopying, recording, or any information storage and retrieval system, without written permission which should be sought from the Copyright Administrator, Central Board of Finance of the Church of England, Church House, Great Smith Street, London SW1P 3NZ.

Printed in England by Rapier Press Ltd

CONTENTS

	page
FOREWORD	iv
INTRODUCTION	1

PART ONE – SETTING THE SCENE

What is Evangelism?	3
An Anglican Way of Evangelism	4
Evangelism and Social Concern	7
Some Marks of the Decade	9

PART TWO – THE DECADE AND THE LOCAL CHURCH

Natural Diffidence	12
Renewal of Life	13
Renewal of Understanding and Confidence	14
Renewal through Prayer and Worship	15
Renewal of Leadership	16
Understanding the Local Community	17
Making Plans	19
A Church-centred Strategy	20
A World-centred Strategy	22
Evangelists, Missions and Special Events	24

PART THREE – WORKING TOGETHER

The Deanery and Local Ecumenical Groups	25
The Diocese and Regional Groups of Churches	27
The Churches at National Level	29
The Churches at International Level	31

PART FOUR – HARD QUESTIONS

What is the Good News for today?	33
How can we communicate the Good News effectively?	34
Apologetics – or How can we argue for the Gospel?	35
Should we change the parish system?	36
What should be our attitude to people of other faiths?	37
What lifestyle does the Gospel require?	38
How should the Decade affect leadership training?	39

QUESTIONS FOR DISCUSSION	42
APPENDIX - Resource Agencies, Books and Courses	44
NOTES	50

FOREWORD BY THE ARCHBISHOP OF CANTERBURY

It was at the 1988 Lambeth Conference that the Anglican Communion was called to make the 1990s a *Decade of Evangelism*. The initiative came primarily from bishops in the developing world who felt, not without reason, that their colleagues in the West failed to give the same priority to evangelism as they did in their own ministries.

This booklet will be of great service to those who have natural hesitations about the Decade. It begins by describing what an Anglican approach to evangelism might imply. It ends by describing a number of 'hard questions' that need to be tackled at national and local level concerning church life, structure and ministerial training.

The Decade of Evangelism has not been inaugurated so that the Church might engage in some novel activity. Rather, we are called to give particular attention to a feature of the Church's life which is essential if the Gospel is to be preached at all, and which needs fresh energy and vision. Whenever I hear that nothing much is happening in this Decade, I recall that the dioceses and parishes of the Church of England, as well as the congregations of other churches (for this is an ecumenical decade), have initiated hundreds of projects, programmes and audits. This booklet describes a number of them and presents a vision of the wide range of possibilities which exist to help our Church in its task of 'making Christ known'.

I believe that this booklet will be of immense service to clergy, members of parochial church councils and congregations working out the implications of the Decade of Evangelism in each local community. There is both advice and challenge contained in these pages. The General Synod Board of Mission is responsible for taking a lead in partnership with the dioceses in sharing plans and ideas for the Decade, and so it is particularly appropriate that this booklet should be written by Canon Philip King, the Board's Secretary. Others will share with me gratitude to Philip for doing this work on our behalf.

†George Cantuar

INTRODUCTION

The Decade of Evangelism or Evangelisation was launched in England on Epiphany Sunday, January 6th 1991. Over 100,000 members of the different denominations attended special services and events to pray for grace and wisdom in *making Christ known*.

Because the emphasis has been upon local, rather than national initiatives information on progress has inevitably been dispersed. Hence one of the needs for this handbook. One diocesan adviser prefaced his report on the first year with the words 'a great deal is happening'. Another diocesan leader has declared 'Probably the most important contributions do not carry a Decade label at all. For what the Decade has done is to make us put Mission at the top of the Agenda of everything that we do. Hardly a committee meets without Mission, or Evangelism appearing as an Agenda item. This applies as much to the Fabric Committee and the Finance Committee as to other committees'.

It is a handbook that is written from a Church of England perspective by the Secretary to the General Synod Board of Mission. It has been written with the encouragement of the Board and its chairman, and with the help of Board members and staff, but the responsibility for its contents is entirely that of its author.

Questions for use in discussion groups and details of Resource Agencies, Books and Courses can be found at the end. Scripture quotations are from the New International Version unless otherwise stated.

PHILIP KING
Secretary to the Board of Mission
Church House, Westminster

THE LAMBETH CALL

'This Conference, recognising that evangelism is the primary task given to the Church, asks each province and diocese of the Anglican Communion, in co-operation with other Christians, to make the closing years of this millenium a "Decade of Evangelism" with a renewed and united emphasis on *making Christ known* to the people of his world'.

Resolution 43 of The Lambeth Conference of Anglican Bishops 1988.

'The pressing needs of today's world demand that there be a massive shift to a "mission" orientation throughout the Communion. The bishop would then become more than ever a leader in mission, and the structure of dioceses, local churches, theological training, etc. would be so reshaped that they would become instruments that generate missionary movement as well as pastoral care.'

Lambeth Conference Report, *The Truth Shall Make You Free*, p.32.

A STATEMENT FROM THE CHURCH OF ENGLAND DECADE STEERING GROUP

During the Decade of Evangelism the Churches are challenged to work together to *make Christ known* to the people of his world:

    praying for the renewing love and power of the Holy Spirit;

    equipping all Christians to live and share the Gospel;

    exploring God's activity in different situations and cultures;

    changing where necessary the Church's worship, ministry and structures;

    confronting injustice and responding to human need.

PART ONE – SETTING THE SCENE

What is Evangelism?

The word 'evangelism' triggers off a variety of responses from the positive to the extremely negative. For some 'it conjures up images of pushy, flashy men with broad forced smiles, straight white teeth and big black Bibles. It triggers pictures of mouths without ears, emotions without reasons, confidence without questions, and religion with a price tag'.[1] No wonder some have been tempted to speak of a 'Decade of Renewal', rather than of a 'Decade of Evangelism'. But a few unfortunate examples do not give us the excuse to ignore the New Testament's call to evangelise any more than a few disastrous development programmes should stop us from giving help to the Third World. In the following pages we shall look at some helpful and sensitive approaches to evangelism and examine its place in the Church of England and its relationship to social action.

The verb 'to evangelise' simply means to 'announce good news'. It comes in Jesus' first sermon at Nazareth when he declares the manifesto of his mission – 'The Spirit of the Lord is upon me, because he has chosen me to *bring good news* to the poor. He has sent me to proclaim liberty to the captives and recovery of sight to the blind; to set free the oppressed and announce that the time has come when the Lord will save his people' (Luke 4.18-19 GNB).

Not all are called to preach, however, and for many of us 'announcing the good news' will usually take the form of discerning and seeking to answer the questions that others have about the faith. Sometimes the real questions are hidden behind the spoken ones. One of our tasks during the Decade will be to encourage and train Christians to discern the questions and sensitively give the answers – with clarity, confidence and courtesy.

'Always be prepared', said St Peter 'to give an answer to everyone who asks you to give the reason for the hope that you have. But do this with gentleness and respect' (1 Peter 3.15-16.). Peter's own experience made him realise that we all lack courage when it comes to witness. His words suggest that evangelism means being prepared to relate 'the good news' to the issues that people are facing, rather than having some slick formula that is used uniformly and mechanically on every occasion.

A clergyman working on a housing estate that had seen a lot of violence commented 'the main deprivation here is lack of hope'. We have to wrestle with the question 'what would bring hope to the people around and how does our hope in God relate to their needs?'

Peter's phrase also implies that we should be living the sort of life that prompts questions. The wrong kind of lifestyle can not only inhibit questions it can undermine the credibility of the answers. It is counter-productive to speak of good news while living bad news.

The Church of England report *The Measure of Mission* puts it this way 'Evangelism is the making known of the Gospel of the Lord Jesus Christ, especially to those who do not know it......We are charged to communicate that the life, death and resurrection of Jesus Christ is good news from God. Evangelism usually involves the use of words, but not necessarily so'.[2] The report later describes the sending of the Son by the Father in the power of the Holy Spirit 'as Saviour of the world' (1 John 4.14), 'as the expiation for our sins' (1 John 4.10) and as the source of new life (John 10.10).[3]

An Anglican Way of Evangelism

Evangelism tends to be something that the Church of England leaves to others. Given our history this is understandable. The seventeenth-century Book of Common Prayer assumes that most of the population will bring their children for baptism; the England of that period was, in this sense at least, a Christian country. Bishop Stephen Neill described the typical English village at the time of the Reformation in these words 'all are baptised Christians, compelled to live more or less Christian lives under the brooding eye of parson and squire. In such a context "evangelisation" has hardly any meaning'.[4] As a result the Anglican model has been pastoral, rather than missionary.

This tradition has both strengths and weaknesses. It is no longer true in many parishes that the majority, or even a significant minority, bring their children for baptism. In 1970 only 347,000 brought their children to the font; by 1987 it had dropped to 233,000. A survey conducted in 1955 showed that 83 per cent of adults over 16 claimed to have attended Sunday School or Bible Class for several years in their childhood. A further 11 per cent had attended for a short time and only 6 per cent had never attended. Probably two-thirds of the nation's children were in Sunday Schools in the 1930s and the 1940s. But the 1989 English Church Census revealed that on a typical Sunday only 14 per cent of children under 15 were in a church related activity of any denomination.[5]

These statistics have implications both for the importance of evangelism and for our approach. We can no longer assume that the majority of those outside the church will have a basic knowledge of the Christian story.

Incidentally not all the current trends are depressing and there is evidence that the decline has been halted. In 1976 the Church of England had 635,000 communicants; by the end of 1991 the average was 726,000.

Because the situation over the last three centuries has so drastically changed we need to heed the call of the Lambeth bishops for 'a shift to a dynamic missionary emphasis going beyond care and nurture to proclamation and service'.[6] It would not be right, however, to become so missionary that we cease to be pastoral. Lord Runcie has said 'Our tradition is to cast evangelism in the mould of pastoral care. For us there has been no sharp divide between preaching the gospel and shepherding souls...ours is not a church with hard edges.... Only when the evangelist becomes the good shepherd whose voice the sheep know will the essentially personal nature of evangelism stand out'.[7]

An 'Anglican way of evangelism' will therefore be both pastoral and missionary and will recognise that for many people conversion is a process rather than a crisis, or that where there are crises they often take place within a process. It is arguable that this was so for the Twelve Apostles.

The relationship of process and crisis can be illustrated by the story of a man who came to faith in prison. He had attended Sunday School as a child, but had drifted away as a teenager. He later came to be married in church and started coming to worship regularly. Then he drifted away again, and was sent to prison after stabbing someone in a fight. In prison he was befriended by a prison visitor and came to a deep, personal faith. The story also illustrates how the ministry of the church through Sunday School and Marriage can be used as stepping stones to faith. The same is true of the other 'occasional offices' – baptisms and funerals.

Evangelism is not solely or even primarily large 'crusades' and 'missions', open-air services or knocking at people's doors. Many congregations who are understandably nervous or suspicious of 'evangelism' may in fact already be engaged in it, through the normal life and ministry of the church and its members. But all of us need to witness more effectively in deed and word and to find ways of reaching toward the majority of the people around us who have little or no experience of Church or even of what the Christian story is all about.

An 'Anglican way of evangelism' will work from an understanding of the church that is open and comprehensive, rather than closed and exclusive. It makes charitable assumptions and assumes people are 'in' until they demonstrate that they are 'out'. Most clergy find it very difficult, for example, to forecast with accuracy which of their confirmation candidates will continue as adult members of the Church.

This approach will use bridges into the community. A less dramatic story than the one above concerns a teacher who found faith after offering to help in a local church's summer playscheme. Initially she found the songs and prayers made her uncomfortable, but she was impressed by the church members she met – 'Instead of finding sombre faces, dressed in "Sunday bests" I met ordinary yet warm, friendly and happy people who made me feel very welcome. The love and warmth that the group showed drew me to wonder if they had actually got something that I was missing out on. Could they be right and I was wrong about their faith in God?' Eventually she came to faith herself.[8]

In many areas the local church has a significant fringe and can combine both a pastoral and missionary approach. In others – in Urban Priority Area (UPA) parishes, for example – there are no longer the same number of opportunities provided by baptisms and weddings and no obvious 'fringe'. But in all contexts the Anglican approach will be one of the Incarnation, an approach that seeks to 'to renounce evangelism by inflexible slogans, and instead to involve ourselves sensitively in the real dilemmas of people.'[9] Archbishop Ramsey called for a readiness to go out and put ourselves 'with loving sympathy inside the doubts of the doubting, the questions of the questioners, and the loneliness of those who have lost the way'.[10]

It is important to speak of an 'Anglican way of evangelism' in order to put right the negative images that some have of the exercise, but this is not to suggest that a sensitive, pastoral approach is not found in other denominations, nor that those of us in the Church of England always remember to be sensitive.

At the same time it would not be accurate to suggest that every other church has a strong emphasis on evangelism. A Greek Orthodox priest working in London visited a friend in Moscow, taking with him an English-Russian dictionary. The friend came to meet him, armed with a Russian-English one. They found it instructive to note the differences between the two; the Russian-English dictionary, for example, had no word for 'mission'. During the Decade we shall need to make sure that we all have 'mission' and 'evangelism' in our dictionaries, and with appropriate definitions.

The Bishop of Ely put it this way in an article in *Theology* called 'An Anglican Theology of Evangelism'[11] – 'Despite an honoured tradition of Evangelicalism we have not been the most evangelistically minded of Churches....I believe this present decade is an opportunity for us corporately to study and acknowledge the strengths and weaknesses of our tradition with a view to deepening our grasp upon evangelism'.

Evangelism and Social Concern

Some are cautious about a Decade of Evangelism because they know of instances where evangelism has become an alternative to social action. There are certainly instances in history where religion has become the 'opiate of the people' and where church growth has been promoted at the expense of social concern. It has been argued that some landowners in the Caribbean were delighted at the spread of the gospel among the slave population on the grounds that it would engender 'a spirit of obedience, humility and diligence'.[12] But the growth of liberation theology in Latin America and the involvement of church members in some of the recent events in Eastern Europe, to take just two examples, suggest that when properly understood the gospel is the opposite of an opiate. To evangelise is to announce good news. This good news is about change in society as well as in individuals, and how to live more justly with other people in one world. The kingdom which Jesus announced in his manifesto sermon at Nazareth is about the whole of life (Luke 4.16-19.). We restrict it if we confine it to personal and churchly concerns.

The Lambeth call is to 'make Christ known', but the Christ we make known must be a Christ who is concerned with the needs of society and of the world, and not just with the church. His 'Great Commission' is a command to make disciples of all nations (Matthew 28.19), but this must mean disciples of Christ and his kingdom and not just disciples of the local Christian community. This is why Dr. Abraham defines evangelism as 'initiating into the kingdom of God'.[13] The story of Zacchaeus is a good example of how repentance and personal commitment to Christ can lead to redistribution of wealth for the good of others.(Luke 19). Christian discipleship applies to how we use resources personally and how we work at pressing those in power to use resources justly.

Bishop Lesslie Newbigin has put it this way 'conversion ....is not a private peace while the whole world goes to rot...it is being caught up into God's action of kingdom. It is being changed so that we can be agents of change'.[14] The Church of England's Decade Steering Group appropriately speaks of the work of making Christ known as including 'confronting injustice and responding to human need' (see page 2).

Another way of expressing the relationship of evangelism and social action is to say that the Great Commission to make disciples is a circle inside the larger circle of the Great Commandment (John 13.34) to love one another. The exact relationship of evangelism and social action will usually depend on the context. We have to ask 'what does love suggest is the priority in the circumstances?' It has been well said that 'a hungry man has no ears'; the first action of love towards a hungry man will therefore be to provide bread, but it will not be the last if we discover the meaning of not living 'by bread alone' (Luke 4.4). People need life, but they also need a reason and a hope for living.

One parish demonstrated how social action can be combined with building friendship by opening a much needed launderette. They didn't bombard customers with gospel tracts, but they did create an opportunity for people to make contact.

Another congregation, meeting on a deprived housing estate in the North-West, worked with others in the community to lobby the local Council for improvements to the estate. The Council were unhelpful, the lobbying became protracted and many gave up the struggle. However the local Christians kept at it – 'it was our faith that made us stick' they said. They demonstrated how the gospel can bring the motivation and the sticking power for social change.

Some Marks of the Decade

As we look at the Lambeth Conference Report (*The Truth Shall Make You Free*) we can detect a number of characteristics which can be expressed in terms of 'marks'. Four are listed here.

The first mark is that the Decade needs to start with the *Local*. Some have expected a comprehensive national programme to be sent down from 'on high'. This would be wrong in principle and unworkable in practice. Early on in the Decade, Nigel McCulloch, Bishop of Wakefield and Chairman of the Church of England Decade Steering Group, said that every parish should work out its strategy in a way 'authentic to its own tradition'. Parishes differ in their churchmanship, their stage of development, and their sociological setting; approaches that are relevant in suburbia may not be relevant in the countryside or on an urban housing estate.

Starting with the local does not mean being limited to the local. It has to be balanced by the mark *co-operative*. The Lambeth call asks every diocese in co-operation with other Christians to have a united emphasis on making Christ known to the people of his world. The deanery and the diocese have a role in helping parishes to be open to fresh ideas and there are a number of regional and national initiatives already planned, as we shall see from part three below.

Wherever possible it is important to work ecumenically, especially as all the churches linked to the ecumenical body 'Churches Together in England' have committed themselves to the Decade.

As far as Roman Catholics and Anglicans are concerned the Decade has a global dimension as well. Part Three describes how we have much to learn from third world churches, both where numbers are fast increasing as well as where Christians are persecuted as a small minority. In several cases persecution has led to growth.

A third mark is to be *comprehensive*. The 44th resolution of the Lambeth Conference called for 'a shift to a dynamic missionary emphasis....' and accepted 'the challenge this presents to diocesan and local church structures and patterns of worship and ministry'.[15] The work of education, training for ministry and social responsibility will all change as they shift in this new direction. Evangelism is not narrow, but comprehensive.

We can only achieve this through the fourth mark – to be *reflective*. There is, of course, the danger of a theological reflection that becomes a safe alternative to action and ends in what Lord Coggan has described as 'analysis paralysis'. It is equally dangerous to have an unreflective activism.

It is important to research into how people come to faith[16] and what people believe. It has been estimated that only 10 per cent of the population of Great Britain are atheists, (though some would say 15 per cent), that 4.5 per cent belong to Other Faiths, and between 9.5 per cent and 10 per cent are churchgoers. Roughly another 25 per cent have some experience of church and some knowledge of the Christian message, without regularly going to church. About half the population have a form of 'religion', believing in some kind of 'god' and turning to prayer on at least special occasions. Such 'religion' may include a mixture of beliefs – reincarnation, 'new age', astrology and superstition – as well as the idea that God is love or that God is paying us out for our sins. One of the tasks during the Decade is to discover what people believe, and what ways there are of clearing away obstacles to the Christian faith. People's beliefs are sometimes a bridge and sometimes a barrier to Christian faith.

Theological reflection is also needed on what the Good News is for young people, for ethnic minorities, the elderly or those disillusioned by the 'enterprise culture' but caught up in it. Questions need to be asked about church life, its worship and its style of leadership. Some of these questions are raised in the following pages and are tackled in the Church of England report *Good News in our Times.*

PART TWO – THE DECADE AND THE LOCAL CHURCH

There are a large number of books and booklets on the subject of evangelism and the local church. Reference to resources is made in the Appendix. This section seeks to set out some principles without too much detail.

Natural Diffidence

Many inside the church are uncomfortable with 'evangelism'. There may be the kind of misunderstanding described in Part One. There may be other reasons as well. Many are shy by nature and feel that religion is a private matter, not something to be shared in conversation. In some families religion has been a cause of argument and division so the subject is avoided. In some social groupings discussion of religion and politics is banned in order to avoid conflict.

There is often a lack of confidence about the faith – 'what is it I'm supposed to believe?' 'How does it square with science?' 'How could I ever answer difficult questions?' It has been well said that the line between belief and unbelief runs through us all. We cannot assume that all those inside the church have 100 per cent faith or that those outside have 100 per cent unbelief.

There may be the comments expressed from outside the church, but often echoed inwardly – 'They're no better than we are'..'who does she think she is to tell us what to believe' .....'The church is full of hypocrites'.

These issues are with us all the time and the Decade can prompt us to deal with them more effectively.

The idea that the church is full of hypocrites is fed by media stories about treasurers who run off with the collection or about Vicars who run off with the organist's wife. Most of us are only too conscious that we fall far short of Christ's ideals. We feel like a salesman with a grubby shirt trying to advertise washing powder. But if we have found forgiveness and help to start again we have something to offer people who might find the same needs in themselves.

This is why one of the best definitions of evangelism is the one that describes it as 'one beggar telling another where they can both find bread'. We share the good news of new life, not from a position of superiority, but as those who equally need forgiveness and renewal.

Another analogy is that of patients in a hospital. We cannot criticise the NHS simply on the grounds that the hospitals are full of people who are ill – we would, however, be justified in asking some critical questions if none of them improve. We cannot wait until we are perfect before we seek to witness to the Good News – the early church didn't. But our witness will be more credible if we can demonstrate the fruits of the Gospel in our lives. It has been well said that 'new Christians are made by Christians being made new'.

Renewal of Life

Both the individual and the congregation need to seek renewal of life in order to engage in credible evangelism. The first question an individual has to ask is 'Am I the Good News or the bad news?' An honest answer will lead to regular prayer, self-examination, repentance and renewal. Our goal is to live the kind of life that is so attractive that people begin to ask us questions about our faith. St Francis said to his followers 'Go and preach the Gospel. If necessary use words'. Modern models can be found in Mother Theresa and Terry Waite, whose commitment to others is a demonstration of the Gospel.

The call is not to a narrow or gloomy holiness. Jesus called us to be 'the light of the world' and 'the salt of the earth'. Salt draws out the flavour of life. He said of himself 'I have come that they may have life, and have it to the full' (John 10.10).

A prayer from Namirembe diocese in Uganda sums it up -

> Holy Spirit give us faith
>
> Holy Spirit give us hope
>
> Holy Spirit give us love
>
> Revive thy work in this land
>
> beginning with me.[17]

The second question, to be asked by a congregation as a whole, is 'Is our church the sort of place we are happy to invite our friends to?' 'Is it warm, attractive and newcomer friendly? What does our church life and worship look like to a total stranger?' A couple who were members of a middle class congregation invited their neighbours to church and grew more and more uncomfortable as they saw them sitting with an air of bewilderment, trying to find their way through a 1,000 page prayer book. The service seemed to have few points of relevance to a newcomer. The inviting couple realised for the first time some of the barriers.

As the report *Evangelism in the Countryside* put it 'A well-kept and welcoming church may itself be evangelistic'.[18] Finance to improve the attractiveness and warmth of a building may be hard to come by[19] and many congregations are resistant to modernisation of worship. Some of our goals may need to be long-term ones. But whatever the form of worship we can work for reality and relevance – these can be present in traditional as well as in modern worship. We can aim, too, for friendliness and welcome. Some congregations have established 'welcome teams' who look out for newcomers. In our British culture our welcomes need to be friendly without being overwhelming. Members can get to know each other better through the availability of coffee after worship, through the development of housegroups, and by encouraging members to 'practise hospitality' (Romans 12.13). Church life with fellowship, hospitality and Communion at its heart can be good news for people who feel a lack of worth or value. One congregation which arranged a number of 'coffee and mince pies' events in members' homes just before Christmas discovered that the events created and deepened neighbours' relationships well beyond the confines of the church. In some areas the Church is one of the few remaining centres of community.

Renewal of Understanding and Confidence

If we are to be 'always prepared to give an answer' we need a renewal of understanding and confidence in order to become more effective in discerning the questions and putting our faith into words. Today's educational methods emphasise learning by participation. The sermon has an important place in worship but it is inadequate as the main means of developing Christian knowledge.

The test of our teaching programme is whether people have so understood and applied the Good News that they are able to communicate it to others in such a way that those others can apply and communicate it too. (2 Timothy 2.2). In congregations where a significant percentage regularly read books, the church bookstall has a useful role in displaying literature that will help church members to develop their understanding and to be able to answer others' questions.

A parish in the Midlands has developed a course entitled 'Good News Down the Street' that has now been used in many parts of the country.[20] It is a series of straightforward Bible Studies on the Gospels, designed for a home setting where church members meet with others and are given the opportunity to explain their faith in a natural and sensitive way.

Several dioceses have produced courses. The Sheffield ones have used the titles 'Something to Share', 'Know your Neighbour' and 'Know your World'.

Continual exhortation to evangelise without giving people the confidence, the motivation and the skills can result in depression and unproductive guilt. People become caught in a trap, one jaw of which is guilt and the other powerlessness. The Diocese of Chichester has produced a course that is designed to release us from this trap. It is called 'Before We Go.'[21] Church members are given the opportunity to share their faith with one another in informal house groups – they then develop the confidence to share their faith more widely.

Renewal through Prayer and Worship

Motivation comes pre-eminently through our experience of Christ in prayer and worship. Bishop John V. Taylor has described witness as 'praise that is overheard'. Perhaps the greatest motivation for evangelism is a thankful and praising heart. Paul's letters are full of thanks and praise. He says 'Devote yourselves to prayer, being watchful and thankful'. He then continues 'pray for us, too, that God may open a door for our message' (Col.4.2-3). Witness is like a flowing stream coming from the spring of a worshipping heart. It is instructive to see the link in the Acts of the Apostles between the filling of the Spirit through prayer and worship and the receiving of confidence and motivation to witness (see 1.14 and 2.1ff; 4.23-31). As a result Peter and John can say even in the middle of persecution and threats 'We cannot help speaking about what we have seen and heard' (Acts 4.20).

Worship provides an opportunity for renewal and a motivation for evangelism, but it can in itself be a proclaiming of the Gospel. The Eucharist is described as a proclamation of the death of Christ (1 Cor.11.26). Bishop Michael Nazir-Ali[22] tells the story of a visitor to Moscow in the '50s who asks a Russian Orthodox priest to describe his church in one sentence. 'It is the church which celebrates the divine liturgy' was the reply. When other forms of communicating the gospel were forbidden many came to faith through attendance at the Liturgy. The report *Evangelism in the Countryside* says that 'Good, appropriate worship, well put together and conducted is a high priority in rural evangelism'.[23] Prayer is often included in the programme of house groups, but many congregations have also encouraged the development of groups that major on prayer and intercession. These vary a great deal in form and style. One example that is designed to be specifically evangelistic is the 'Prayer Triplets' scheme. As its title suggests members of the congregation meet in threes for half an hour or more each week in order to pray that specific friends and contacts may come to faith.[24]

Renewal of Leadership

A Methodist study on why churches grow[25] identified five reasons. A fresh look at worship and a special emphasis on evangelism in the programme were two, but the others directly involved the style of leadership:

> the quality of pastoral oversight; this oversight might include the ministry of pastoral visitors and others, and not just that of the minister;

a ministry which relates to people at every phase of life and especially at the major life events;

and a collaborative style of leadership with both ministers and laity sharing responsibility together.

Effective leadership is critical to motivation and encouragement in evangelism. Not all clergy have had adequate experience and training in mobilising others and many congregations are only too happy to 'leave it all to the Vicar' especially when it comes to sharing faith. In some parishes there is little evidence of vision, goal-setting or leadership. At the other extreme there are examples where 'strong' leadership has brought about rapid change without adequate consultation or with only a pretence at consultation. At first there seem to be good results, but soon many of the congregation begin to grumble and then become alienated. They did not feel involved in the decision-making and so do not 'own' the goals and programme of the leadership; as a result they are unwilling to volunteer for tasks and eventually the leaders complain 'we are always left to do everything; no-one seems ready to help'.

Questions also need to be asked about the appropriate style of leadership for different settings, cultures and stages of development. What may be appropriate for suburban parishes may not be appropriate for rural or urban priority areas.[26]

Understanding the Local Community

Over recent years the Church has increasingly learnt the value of 'market research'. There are various approaches that are often described under the somewhat forbidding title of 'Mission Audit'. We think of auditors as those who check on financial income and expenditure but we also need a regular check-up on the use of our non-financial resources for mission. It is also helpful to remember that the word 'audit' has the idea of listening – we need to listen to the hopes and needs of the community around.

A Mission Audit is a way of helping a congregation to plan for the future by investigating the present. It is a process of diagnosis followed by prescription. Some congregations do very little by way of strategic planning, while some fall into the equally dangerous trap of planning without careful research, consultation and prayer. An audit can be enormously enlightening both for leaders and members. Even regular members may find it difficult to give a newcomer details of children's and youth organisations, crèche facilities and local schools.

Most audit systems provide simple methods of asking questions about the church and about the local community, comparing the two by age, sex, social and ethnic background, etc. The process can bring encouragement and reassurance as well as challenge. One church discovered that it had a good number of people in their twenties and a good number of older people, but that there was an unexplained gap in between. It then discovered that there was the same gap in the population at large, mainly because there were few large houses in the area and it therefore catered for young couples with small families or older couples whose children had grown up and left home. Another church discovered that it was catering for young people who were likely to do A levels, but not for the many young people in the area who were likely to leave school at 16.

Another undertook a survey of what had been thought of as a 'retirement village' only to find that 70 per cent were under 40. One church plotted the homes of its members on a large map and noticed that very few came from a large housing estate on the edge of the parish. The same church used the map to plot leisure centres, shops, clubs, pubs, industries and work places; they were also able to pinpoint where several members of the congregation worked.

The leaders of one congregation were discussing how to make contact with the staff of a local hospital and then discovered that three members of their congregation worked there.

This data is essential in planning how to re-deploy our energies and resources for mission.

As we shall see below there is added value when audits are conducted in partnership with other local churches, through a deanery or a local council

of churches. In rural areas links can be made with the 'village appraisals' recommended by the Department of the Environment.

Audits can be extended to include questions on how people view their neighbourhood, asking about both the good points and the drawbacks. Some include sensitive questions about people's beliefs; wisely handled this kind of research, conducted in a shopping area or door to door, can lead into faith discussions.

The list of possibilities is endless; there are details of a number of mission audits in the appendix.

Making Plans

> if you fail to plan
> you plan to fail

There are a number of dangers to be avoided in the Mission Audit process. Three are mentioned here.

The first danger is that if the process is badly planned or handled it can end in depression rather than in vision and encouragement. It is important to look for positive points of encouragement in both church and community.

The second is where the research is not followed up by action. It is important to end up by setting a series of simple goals and objectives. These will obviously vary from church to church. Goals need to be specific, realistic, measurable and achievable. Goals that are unrealistic lead only to depression.

The third danger is that of ending up with a long list of possibilities for action which are simply added on to the present programme. There is a need to prioritise – to decide which possibilities are the most strategic, urgent and achievable, and what parts of the present programme should be phased out. Some churches already have far too much going on and need to prune the number of committee and other meetings so that church members have time for their families and time to build friendships with neighbours and others in the community. A couple in the Midlands who joined a busy church later exclaimed 'We started coming five years ago and now we have virtually no friends outside the church'.

There may be an overworked 'core group' who need help in sharing leadership and ministry with a wider circle. Larger churches may need a 'ministry co-ordinator', ordained or lay, who has the skills of 'Recognising, distributing and co-ordinating the ministry of others'.[27]

It is also important to timetable; some new ideas may need to be introduced over a period of years.

A Church-centred Strategy

A number of goals will be 'church-centred'. It may be a matter of finding and training two more Sunday School teachers, starting a Parent and Toddler group, creating a social group for 'singles', beginning a Family Service, or setting up a house group on a housing estate. In some churches there may be not be the possibility of any of these things; the first aim may be to deepen friendships by encouraging the growth of hospitality within the congregation or to find some way of welcoming those who are newcomers to the district. Several parishes have prepared 'Welcome Packs' for new arrivals in the area, giving details of local amenities, the doctors' surgeries, bus services, etc. Added to this is a copy of the parish magazine and details of church activities.

Many congregations have adapted, enlarged or developed their 'plant' in order to be of service to the wider community. One church in the East End of London was able to pull down its old, dilapidated building and with the help of a Christian charity build in its place a modern community centre which includes an area for congregational worship. The centre is a hive of activity, including a coffee bar, a sports hall, a keep fit gymnasium, and a number of rooms used for such activities as English classes for ethnic

minority groups. In this particular instance the dimension of social service is paramount and evangelism is a possibility rather than a programme. There are many examples where congregations have adapted and transformed their buildings, without going so far as demolition – either because it was felt unnecessary or because the building was 'listed' as of architectural importance. A Durham example is described by the Archbishop of Canterbury in his book *The Church in the Market Place*.

Another way of tackling the problem of a church building which is 'remote' either geographically or culturally can be illustrated from the experience of the parish of Chester-le-Street. The parish created a number of different groups, made up of church members living on the housing estates surrounding the town. The former strategy of drawing people to 'come' to the parish church demanded the crossing of a cultural barrier in order to enter an atmosphere that was 'posh' and therefore alien. It had been of limited effectiveness as a result. The new congregations met in schools, clubs and in one case in a pub. They were involved in social action as well as in worship.[28]

The Chester-le-Street examples are often described as 'churchplanting'. There are a growing number of congregations who are 'planting' groups from among their members in schools and halls; in some cases there has been a plant into part of another parish. There are also instances of a 'transplant' in order to revive a struggling congregation. These need, of course, to be undertaken with the approval of the bishop and other local church leaders. Examples can be found in the report of a 1991 churchplanting conference under the title *Planting New Churches*.

A worship service or event is not necessarily the most appropriate first contact with those outside the church. Some congregations have established enquiry groups called 'Looking for God' or 'Agnostics Anonymous'. Others have established catechumenate and nurture groups that cater for those on the fringe of church life.

A World-centred Strategy

It would be wrong to think of the Decade as simply or even mainly an exercise to draw people into church buildings. The illustrations of light and salt in the Sermon on the Mount (Matthew 5.13-16) suggest an emphasis of going out to penetrate and transform society. The church is present through its individual members in different workplaces, community groups and leisure pursuits. One of the tasks of the Decade is to help individual Christians to relate their faith to the issues they encounter in these places, and to look for new opportunities to enter others' worlds, just as Christ has done. The Decade Steering Group statement quoted on p.2 speaks of 'exploring God's activity in different situations and cultures'.

A true layperson is one 'whose centre is outside the church'.[29] The different spheres of life where the people of God can bear witness include

- family and friends, near and far
- neighbours and the local community
- places of work, whether paid or voluntary
- community service groups
- politics and trade unions
- social clubs, sports and leisure groups

In all the above spheres the Christian aims to witness by simply being there, by lifestyle, by involvement, by speech and by action. Some are like Cynthia who works in a Body Shop; because she is known to be a Christian people come up to her to discuss life's questions and personal issues. Some are like Madge who found her neighbours were suspicious of a newcomer and managed to get him accepted by others in the street when she took the lead and invited him into her home. He repaired one of her windows in exchange for a hot dinner.

In his book *The Gap* Jack Burton, an ordained Methodist minister and bus driver, recommends that congregations should identify 'focal points' in the community and help their members to enter them. 'Public houses, social clubs, youth centres, gardening clubs, political centres, protest movements – wherever people assemble in such a manner that an impact is made on the community we should aim to have somebody present'.[30]

The Lambeth call is to make Christ known, but the Christ we make known should not be the Christ of an ecclesiastical ghetto, but a Christ who is concerned and involved with every dimension of life. For some, like Cynthia and Madge, this will need no special training; for others it will.

There are many ways in which the local and the wider church can help individuals and groups in relating the good news of the Gospel to issues of family life, industry and politics. It can encourage and foster vocations to frontier tasks outside the church and help its members to reckon involvement in industry, whether union or management, in local politics or in community service as important, if not more important, than vocation to serve on the PCC or to the ordained ministry. It can emphasise the need to support a member teaching in a local comprehensive as much as a member called to teach in Africa.

Too often 'lay training' is centred on 'Sunday ministry' rather than on 'Monday ministry'. The main purpose of the organisations of the Church is 'to nourish and train the members of the Church for their work in the world and to uphold them in it'.[31] Some community, industrial and economic issues are so complex that specialist groups are needed – sometimes at regional and national levels. This can be illustrated by the book of essays *The Gospel and Contemporary Culture* published in 1992.

Needless to say the clergy will not necessarily be the best equipped to lead such training exercises, and yet they have an important part to play. There may be the need for discussion groups that include both those who have theological training and those directly involved in industry and in the community. The fruits of these discussions can then be shared more widely.

Christians in the world need training, but they also need support. In one deprived borough the members of a local church recognised that social transformation was impossible without political commitment. Several joined a local political party and one of their members was elected to office in the Borough Council. He meets every week with members of his church in order to think through the Christian perspectives on current issues and to pray.

Not everyone can have a special support group, but it helps if the Sunday worship has a Monday dimension and that members feel that their Monday work is part of their offering to God and their priestly ministry.

The witness of a congregation will lack credibility unless individual members are involved in the life of the local community, but the witness of individuals will in turn lack credibility unless the congregation as a whole is seen to be committed to social transformation. Bishop Lesslie Newbigin has argued that the task of the ministry is to 'lead the congregation as a whole in a mission to the community as a whole, to claim its whole public life, as well as the personal lives of all its people, for God's rule'.[32] Many have rejected the Gospel because it has been perceived as calling for a private and domestic discipleship that means a withdrawal from the world; the church has been seen as an ecclesiastical departure lounge, with its passengers, baggage all packed, waiting for their flight to be called.

Evangelists, Missions and Special Events

Some have reacted against a whole decade of evangelism in the misguided impression that it will mean an exhausting succession of missions and special events. One cartoon showed a tired clergyman on a visit to his doctor and asking the question 'Doctor, do you think I have a decade of evangelism in me?'

However the services of a skilled and experienced evangelist and the planning of special events and missions have an important contribution to make. There are two important caveats. One is to avoid the subtle temptation to '*vica*rious' evangelism, leaving everything to the outside expert. The other is to avoid too great a dependence on a mission or special event. There can be such a flurry of activity that once the event is over people flop back exhausted.

A mission is not a panacea, but properly planned and handled it can provide a valuable peak in a programme of continuous evangelism.

Again it is important to be clear about goals and objectives and to ask what continuing changes in the life and activities of individuals and of the congregation it is designed to achieve. For example some parishes have programmed discussion or enquiry groups set up for a mission in such a way that they can continue afterwards.

The office of evangelist is one that has by and large been neglected in the Church of England. Several dioceses are investigating ways of identifying, training and deploying those who have the gift of an evangelist.

PART THREE – WORKING TOGETHER

In calling for a Decade of Evangelism the Lambeth Bishops urged us to work 'in co-operation with other Christians'. We can do this at local, regional, and national levels and also globally.

The Deanery and Local Ecumenical Groups

For Anglicans the Clergy Chapter and the Deanery Synod provide structures for sharing ideas and strategy. But wherever possible the ideal is to work ecumenically. This is made easier when a Ministers' Fraternal and Local Council of Churches (often now renamed as 'The Churches Together in........') already exist.

In practice both Anglican and Ecumenical networks are important. A significant ingredient in the launch of the Decade was a call to prayer signed by the four Presidents of the new ecumenical instrument for England – 'Churches together in England' (CTE). We can therefore assume that all those associated with CTE will be open to the possibility of co-operating together in evangelism – this will *include* Baptists, many of the Black-led Churches, Methodists, Orthodox, the Roman Catholic Church, the Salvation Army, the Society of Friends and the United Reformed Church.

The Deanery Synod or the Local Council of Churches may be willing to set up a Decade planning group, and to organise a series of training days. One deanery in East Anglia held a day conference and included workshops on worship, working with young families, using the home, and 'bringing in the men'. Some Local Councils of Churches have organised a series of prayer meetings at different times and locations throughout their area. Several are planning Christian Festivals, Missions and other special events.

Ideas have included drama in the shopping centre and a 'Funday' in a local park. Others have organised joint programmes that are not specifically evangelistic, but are related to evangelism – for example a support network for Christian teachers, and a bereavement counselling programme.

The Mission Audit process can be used to research a deanery or local authority area in order to identify special needs and opportunities. There may be a large housing area with few churchgoers and perhaps no church buildings. It may be possible to plan a churchplanting programme in order to set up a Local Ecumenical Project.[33] There may be an industrial complex with no organised Christian witness. It may be possible to identify particular specialists who can be used or models which can be shared more widely. No congregation is able to specialise in everything. One congregation may be strong on youth work, another on bereavement counselling, another on inter-faith dialogue. Sensitive bridge building is needed so that 'successful' congregations can see that they have needs and the 'struggling' feel they have something to share.

One way forward is to have specialist task groups – for children, or for youth, for example. One deanery in a rural area found that lack of numbers, facilities and leaders was hindering youth work and organised a Deanery Youth Day in order to bring encouragement. Workshops and teaching sessions on a Sunday afternoon led into a united evening service.

It may be possible to draw on the help of volunteers who go from one congregation to help another. This has been formalised at national level through organisations which enable young people to give a year of their time to work as volunteers in a local church.[34] In one deanery 30 people were drawn from 15 churches to form faith-sharing teams. Different churches in the deanery allocated the sermon slot to a team. A later development was to use some of the teams in leading missions in the area.

One of the dangers of working co-operatively is that of becoming bogged down in committees. Sometimes an ecumenical committee is set up, but is unable to function because it has to report back at every stage to each of the local churches. One answer is to set up a task group that is allowed a reasonable amount of freedom. Another is to let different churches have the 'lead responsibility' in different projects. In one area the Roman Catholics run the summer holiday club, the Baptists the Good Friday march of witness and the Anglicans the Christian coffee shop.

The Diocese and Regional Groups of Churches

For many Anglicans the diocese is the basic unit of the church. It may be more difficult to work ecumenically at this level, especially when denominational boundaries are not coterminous, but virtually every part of the country is included in a county or metropolitan area ecumenical council.[35]

Most of the illustrations below are from Anglican dioceses, but a number of them can be or are being developed ecumenically. The examples given are for purposes of illustration and do not attempt to be exhaustive. Details in this and other sections are apt to change, but are correct according to the information available at the time of going to press.

Many of the examples of co-operation at local level are also relevant to dioceses and regional groups of churches. There will often be more expertise available at this level for setting up task and study groups and for training consultants.

Prayer A large number of dioceses have produced prayer material and several have organised prayer schools. The Southwell prayer card has the slogan 'Forward and Outward'; the Winchester leaflet focuses on the prayer 'Lord Jesus Christ, Son of God, have mercy upon me a sinner'.

Mission Audit Many dioceses have a mission audit or parish appraisal programme. The Coventry diocese has participated in an ecumenical one produced by The Coventry and Warwickshire Ecumenical Committee (CWEC).

Strategy There are a good number of strategy documents on offer. The one produced by the Bradford evangelism committee has three stages – the formation of the local congregation (1991-3), the development of the Christian community (1994-7) and mission to the local society (1998-2000).

Teaching & Training Resources The Liverpool diocese has a one-year foundation course in Christian believing, Manchester courses on 'Telling His story, your story, and our story' and Guildford a series of leaflets for evangelistic use at baptisms, weddings and funerals. Southwark organised a resources day at the Cathedral, with training workshops. Hereford has a mobile roadshow for parishes and deaneries. A number have produced posters. Chelmsford has a series of ten mission leaflets ranging from sharing in worship and sharing the faith to growth through groups and planning a parish strategy. The Chichester and Sheffield courses are mentioned on page 15. Several have commissioned videos. A good number of training resources are available from voluntary mission agencies. Among the favourites are the Bible Society Video course 'Person to Person'.

Consultants and Task Groups Many of us have difficulty in translating audits and strategy into action. A number of dioceses are training consultants to help parishes in working out their strategy and in setting goals and objectives. Some are training lay evangelists who are then equipped to train others. Hereford has a training programme for laity, while the Edmonton episcopal area in the diocese of London is planning to organise deanery faith-sharing teams of laity.

Conferences and Seminars provide opportunities for consultation, planning and training.

Festivals and Celebrations Ecumenical co-operation is particularly important in planning Christian festivals, celebrations and other events. The Oxford diocese is sharing in the planning of a series of ecumenical public events in 1994 which will be staged in key towns across the area as an exercise in raising the profile of evangelism.

Structures A strategy needs the right structure to make it effective. Most dioceses have found it valuable to identify or recruit an officer for the Decade – usually a diocesan missioner or adviser in evangelism – and to identify or establish a task group to co-ordinate the planning. The task group may report to the Board of Mission, to the Bishop's Council or direct to the Bishop. Whatever the structure it has proved valuable to keep in close liaison with the Social Responsibility and Education Departments, the Pastoral Committee, and with those responsible for providing study and training programmes for clergy and others.

The Salisbury Diocese has brought many of these concerns together in its Mission Audit programme which has units on evangelism, social concern, ministry, pastoral care, belief and sharing with other churches. It then suggests that parishes involved should plan a stewardship programme in order to share plans with the wider church membership.

Lambeth Resolution 44, which calls for changes to structures in order to facilitate a 'dynamic missionary emphasis' is spelt out further in the Mission and Ministry section, in the following words 'The pressing needs of today's world demand that there be a massive shift to a "mission" orientation throughout the Communion. The bishop would then become more than ever a leader in mission, and the structure of dioceses, local churches, theological training, etc. would be so reshaped that they would become instruments that generate missionary movement as well as pastoral care.'[36]

Sector Ministries These structural links make it easier to promote discussion of how the Decade can and should affect the work of sector ministries to industry, hospitals and prisons.

Cathedrals and Historic Churches welcome a large number of tourists and other visitors. Several Cathedral Chapters are considering how the Decade should affect their programmes and help visitors to become pilgrims and then disciples. Some are, for example, producing literature that goes beyond architectural notes and spells out the gospel significance of the font and other parts of the building. Wakefield Cathedral has agreed on a 'mission statement' seeing it as the Cathedral's task 'To ensure that the claims of Christ are presented in those places and among those communities that cannot easily be reached by the Parish Churches...'

The Churches at National Level

Co-ordinating Across the Denominations In 1991 The British Council of Churches was succeeded by a number of new ecumenical bodies for England, Ireland, Scotland and Wales. The one for England is called 'Churches Together in England' – abbreviated to 'CTE'. The umbrella body that embraces all four is 'The Council of Churches for Britain and Ireland' (CCBI). The Co-ordinating Group for Evangelisation was set up as part of CTE and its composition includes representatives from the historic denominations and also from black-led churches and the new churches. It meets regularly to exchange ideas, share resources and give advice on national evangelistic programmes and projects.

Research and Reflection The advantage of having ten years of focus on evangelism is that it provides an opportunity to look carefully at our theology, strategy and practice of evangelism. It is difficult to plan evangelistic strategies unless and until we understand more about the ways in which people come to faith. In 1989 The British Council of Churches sponsored a research project on how people come to faith. Sponsorship has been taken over by CTE with a view to publishing a report by the end of 1992. 'The Gospel and our Culture' project was sponsored by the BCC under the leadership of Bishop Lesslie Newbigin; reference to this project is made on page 35 below.

Courses and Resources The CCBI plan a Lent course in 1994 on the person of Jesus Christ; it is likely to be designed for use by church members as an opportunity for discussion with friends and neighbours outside the church. Often resources produced by one denomination have been used by others. Examples include the Methodist publication *20 things to do during a Decade of Evangelism* and the Church of England report on children's evangelism – *All God's Children?* This report was a joint production by the Boards of Education and Mission, with the help of representatives from other churches and from a number of mission agencies.

There is reference elsewhere in this handbook to the many other examples of research, programmes and resources at national level.

Television and Radio One of the many challenges of the Decade is to explore and develop the potential of radio and television as a means of communicating the Good News.

It is estimated that 60 per cent of the British population watch a religious programme in any given month. One forecast is that there will eventually be up to 400 local and community radio stations and potential for up to 40 cable channels.[37]

A good deal of work has been undertaken already by churches and groups of churches. There are several examples of ecumenical groups who are involved in community radio, but there is a need to develop resources, training and support for current and potential radio producers and presenters.

At least three dioceses have video production units, making it possible to envisage the day when some will be able to produce programmes for local cable channels.

It will be far more demanding in terms of resources and expertise to explore the setting up of a national cable channel for religious programmes. This could only be done ecumenically, assuming it is desirable.

The Churches at International Level

The call for a Decade of Evangelisation came from Pope John Paul VI and the call for a Decade of Evangelism originated in the international 1988 Lambeth Conference of Anglican Bishops. At least as far as Roman Catholics and Anglicans are concerned the Decade is global.

Too often partnership between different Provinces of the Anglican Communion is distorted by finance, so that the relatively affluent are permanently cast into the role of givers and the materially poor into the role of receivers. The Decade is an opportunity to change this pattern. Those who are materially poor are often spiritually rich and have much to share in terms of evangelistic enthusiasm and experience. Worldwide there are 1200 people being added to Anglican churches every day, the majority joining churches in Africa, Asia and Latin America. As the Bishop of Sabah has said 'The Decade of Evangelism offers the opportunity for Third World developing countries to offer much to the work of the Anglican Communion'.

In April 1991 a conference was held for a number of Anglican Primates and representatives of Anglican mission agencies from England, Wales and Ireland. One of the key recommendations was that the church in the West should be helped to recognise its needs and learn to receive. This can be done in a number of ways. One is through the sharing of models and stories. The Anglican Consultative Council includes a number in its regular Newsheet on the Decade. Raymond Fung tells a number of such stories in his book *The Isaiah Vision*. One concerns a group of Christians in Hong Kong who found that women who worked in the local factories were being denied paid maternity leave. They started a campaign to get the situation altered; a number of people outside the church were attracted to join the campaign and some of them were converted.[38]

International sharing also takes place through partnership interchange. The United Society for the Propagation of the Gospel (USPG) and The Church Missionary Society (CMS) have combined with the diocese of Southwark and the Church Commissioners to make a Zambian priest available for an action research programme on inner city evangelism based at a parish in Waterloo, South London. BCMS Crosslinks has made it possible for a Kenyan clergyman and his wife to be seconded to a parish in Manchester. The South American Missionary Society (SAMS) arranged for a visit to England from an Argentine evangelist.

The Spanish Reformed Episcopal Church felt it was appropriate to mark 1992, the five hundreth anniversary of Columbus' arrival in the Americas, by organising an evangelistic project in the Madrid area of Spain with the help of Latin American Anglicans.

The Province of Nigeria has set a remarkable example by consecrating six new missionary bishops to work in primarily Muslim areas. In Mozambique Bishop Denis Sengulane has challenged members of his diocesan synod to lead at least one person to Christ within the year. The Province of Uganda has set out a series of yearly targets for the Decade, starting in the first year with training and retraining and in the second year with outreach to nominal Christians. One important dimension will be the training of clergy in the areas of leadership and in mobilising laity for ministry.

A number of English dioceses are planning to invite overseas partners to share in an audit or in a series of celebration events.

PART FOUR - HARD QUESTIONS

'There is an imperative laid upon the Church today to move again into the unknown, "outside the gate" where hard questions are asked' (paragraph 21 of the Lambeth Mission and Ministry Report).[39]

'What you are really saying', said a deanery synod member at the end of a presentation on the Decade, 'is that we need to do the same things, but better than before'. He was both right and wrong. He was right in the sense that, as we have seen, an Anglican way of evangelism is based on the normal life and witness of a parish church and its members. Work, leisure and community activities can all have an evangelistic dimension, as well of course as Baptisms, Weddings, Funerals, Sunday worship, Parents and Toddlers and the youth group. Sometimes the evangelistic cutting edge has been blunted or is non-existent and we need to live and witness 'better than before'. However a Decade also gives us the opportunity of going further and deeper in order to listen to and ask some hard questions – about the church's message, lifestyle and structures and about the society in which we live.

The following are brief introductions, by way of illustration, to some of the questions that need to be asked. They are designed to give a vision of the possible agenda rather than to give complete answers. The hard questions that the Lambeth Bishops had in mind were probably general questions about life, asked by those outside the church. This section selects a number of 'hard questions' that need to be asked both within the gate and outside it.

What is the Good News for today?

One of the classic debates is between those who believe that the Gospel is an unchanging series of statements that simply has to be transmitted, and those who believe in a process of 'contextualisation' whereby each individual and group is helped to discover what is the good news for them. Few people are at either extreme of the spectrum. Most acknowledge that the process of evangelism requires a linking of 'their story' with 'our story' and 'his story' - i.e. the life, death and resurrection of Jesus Christ and his significance for us.[40]

Even within the pages of the New Testament there are differences in the presentation of the Gospel. Peter presents Christ to a Jewish audience as the Messiah, the fulfilment of Jewish hopes, and bases his arguments on Old

Testament promises (Acts 2). In Athens Paul presents Christ to a Gentile audience as the Lord of life, drawing on material from local poets (Acts 17). Professor C.F.D. Moule argued that the presentation of the Gospel in the early church was to a large extent determined by the background and understanding of the listener. Canon Michael Green has argued that the Gospel had a recognisable shape and content, but that the 'pattern of sound words' was a springboard rather than a straitjacket.[41]

The individuals and groups that we meet today are not likely to be identical with either first-century Jews in Jerusalem, or first-century pagans in Athens. What, for example, is the good news for someone trapped by our modern 'Enterprise Culture'? On the one hand there are those such as middle managers who are pressurised into working long hours under the fear that if they fail to 'get up' an ever-narrowing pyramid they will be forced to 'get out'. On the other hand there are those who have become victims of mechanisation and a shrinking job market and have been forced into redundancy. Both groups feel a sense of powerlessness – that decisions are always made somewhere else. Both groups need to hear the good news that God's sovereignty extends even over economic structures, that he identifies with us in our needs, that he counts us all as having worth and value, and that he has acted and acts to redeem and remake both individuals and structures.[42] There may be some similarities between those trapped in an Enterprise Culture and those in the Greek world of the first century who felt themselves to be at the mercy of forces over which they had no control.[43]

There are many groups in society today that feel marginalised; all need to hear the good news that the gospel has made irrelevant the barriers between race, class, sex and status. (Galatians 3.28) There are those who suffer from emptiness, described by Carl Jung as 'the central neurosis of our time'; like the woman at the well in John 4 they can discover purpose, meaning and fulfilment as well as forgiveness.

How can we communicate the Good News effectively?

Much of our worship and teaching employs words and ideas that are unfamiliar to the majority. Every science and philosophy has some technical phrases that have to be mastered by the newcomer, but in the life of the church it is good to keep these to a minimum, especially as a large percentage of our population do not habitually read. One of the tasks of the Decade will be to discover how to communicate the Gospel in language and in ways that are intelligible and relevant. Communication is not, of course, limited to words. We have a God who has communicated through Creation, through the Scriptures and through his Son, the living Word. Words need to be accompanied by actions and vice versa. This is why the life and fellowship of the local church is so important in demonstrating the Gospel. Congregations become more effective in communicating the gospel when they demonstrate loving relationships and are engaged in social action and reconciliation; this is also true of those that demonstrate the transforming power of the gospel through a ministry of healing.

Apologetics – or How can we argue for the Gospel?

We need to demonstrate the gospel, but we also need, on occasion, to argue for it. The writings of C.S. Lewis are a model in this respect.

'The Gospel and Our Culture' project (see page 29) has been set up to find ways of arguing for the gospel in our modern, secularised culture. In his book *The Gospel in a Pluralist Society* Bishop Lesslie Newbigin has shown that in western society religion is excluded from the 'public world of scientific facts' and relegated to the 'private world of moral and religious opinions'. Our society provides a range of philosophies, religions, cults and ideals; there are for example a variety of attitudes to marriage and family life. We are like shoppers, free to select from the wide choice in the supermarket of ideas. Secularism argues that there is no objective truth with which to test the validity of one set of values or ideas as against another; it is a matter of personal choice. This view is not limited to an intellectual establishment, but has been popularised through the media and has therefore been widely adopted, at least unconsciously. When it comes to the 'public world of scientific facts' the expert, often in a white coat, faces the camera. When it comes to religion or morals there is a debate between opposing views; the implication is that there is no consensus about the truth.

Bishop Newbigin demonstrates that a number of scientific theories are based on hypotheses that are not open to ordinary testing but rely as religion does on the use of a mixture of faith and reason in interpreting experience. This makes possible a dialogue between the Gospel and modern secularised culture.

In 1992 the Project published a collection of essays under the title *The Gospel and Contemporary Culture,* relating the Gospel to science, the arts, knowledge, economics, education, health and the media.

This is just one area, or set of areas, where apologetics is needed today.

Should we change the parish system?

We have already seen (page 28) how the Lambeth Bishops called for a readiness to change the structures of dioceses and local churches in order to 'generate missionary movement as well as pastoral care'. One of the structures in question is the parish system. Some of those who are enthusiastic for churchplanting, for example, feel that the parish system is a hindrance to opportunities for expansion. There are some who want to abolish the system altogether, while others would be content to press for greater flexibility and wider opportunities for experimentation. The worship groups meeting in schools and clubs described on page 21 are an experiment that offers greater flexibility and freedom than is possible in the parish church.

The parish system has less rationale in areas where the population is mobile and can exercise a right of choice. It does, however, have the advantage of providing a congregation with a commitment to a specific geographical area. Those who commute a distance to church tend to have a diminished commitment to the community where they live and can end up as an inward looking fellowship of the like minded. For these reasons some argue for a modification of the structures rather than a revolution. A number of parishes can be grouped together, formally or informally, in order to provide a range of specialities in evangelism. In one inner city area where the number of confirmation candidates was small, but the variety of racial, age and educational backgrounds wide, several parishes worked together to provide a range of specialist preparation classes.

One of the marks of the church is 'catholicity'. It should therefore provide a welcome and a fellowship that transcend all barriers of race, sex, age and background. The ideal of the parish church is that it should provide a welcome for 'all in each place'. Some church growth groups in the United States have, however, argued that evangelism is more effective when people are invited into a 'homogeneous' group whose members are of the same class, age, race or social background. Taken to its logical conclusion this argument could result in racially segregated churches. It is a dangerous path to follow. On the other hand most churches provide specialist groups for children, youth and women. Where there is a varied ethnic mix there may be the need for special congregations, especially where there is an ethnic group whose main language is not English. There are churches in the West Midlands who have an Asian congregation meeting in the same building, but at a different time, from the English speaking congregation. These special congregations are able to use Asian languages and are able to preserve something of their own cultural identity. There are instances in East London where special congregations of this kind are drawn from a wide area, across several parish boundaries.

'Homogeneous' networks, groups and congregations can only be justified, however, where there are very special circumstances; they should be seen as temporary staging posts towards a fully 'catholic' fellowship.

What should be our attitude to people of other faiths ?

This is undoubtedly one of the hardest questions of the Decade. Some have argued that because we live in a multi-faith society it is inappropriate to have a Decade of Evangelism. Certainly there are a number of other faith communities that feel vulnerable and have a folk memory of aggressive evangelism in the past. Awareness of and sensitivity to these feelings is essential.

However we need to get the issue into perspective. Distinctions can be made between the Jewish community which does not believe in seeking converts and is shrinking as a result of secularism and marrying 'out' and the Muslim community which does believe in mission and is growing. In fact most faith traditions, with the exception of Judaism and Jainism, incorporate a sense of mission. But even if we add up all those of other faiths, including nominal adherents, they do not represent more than 4.5 per cent of the population of the United Kingdom. The Jewish community represents perhaps 0.5 per cent. Size is not of course the only measure of importance, but it would be strange to reject the idea of a Decade of Evangelism when about 85 per cent of the population are not committed members of any major faith. Some have argued that on practical grounds we need to concentrate on the 85 per cent. Certainly there is enough to do for a whole Decade with such a large number of people, and it can be categorically stated that there have been no plans drawn up by the historic churches to target those of other faiths as a result of the launch of the Decade.

The Lambeth Conference resolutions concerning other faiths (numbers 20 and 21) use the word 'dialogue' rather than 'evangelism' – perhaps because history includes so many examples of insensitive and even aggressive evangelism. The word 'dialogue' suggests a relationship of equals, with respect for the other partner. Appendix 6 of the Conference report sets out guidelines for dialogue and commends the threefold approach of Understanding, Affirmation (of all that is good in other faiths), and Sharing.

The definition of dialogue in the Board for Mission and Unity's report *The Measure of Mission* is relevant here: '...participants should bear witness to their own beliefs and, when confidence has grown, be ready to challenge and be challenged by others. True dialogue is perfectly compatible with faithful witness, and so in such mutual and honest sharing the possibility of conversion remains'.[44]

The gospel is good news for all and Christians should be prepared to share their faith with all, but with gentleness and respect for the integrity of others. We must be ready to listen and to learn before we speak. Especial sensitivity is required in our dialogue and personal encounters with those of other faiths.

What lifestyle does the gospel require?

What change of lifestyle is required of those who become disciples of Christ? The rich young ruler was asked to give up everything; few evangelists would issue such a challenge today, though logically the lordship of Christ is comprehensive and should affect life in its totality. The story of Zacchaeus, who gave half his goods to the poor and made recompense for his previous extortions is a reminder that if a challenge to discipleship has no socio-economic implications it is open to criticism as an example of what has been described as 'cheap grace'. This phrase implies that God's love and forgiveness are being offered 'on the cheap' without any demands for a change of lifestyle.

On the other hand a long list of demands for change in lifestyle can fall into the opposite trap of obscuring grace by legalism. In some cases the implications of the gospel were worked out gradually. Peter and others were slow to move to a position of welcoming Gentiles; the abolition of slavery took many centuries.

This was one of the many questions that was raised at the 1988 Lambeth Conference. In a paper presented to the conference Bishop David Gitari of Kenya distinguished those things that should be changed straightaway, those customs that were acceptable, and those that should be changed with time. In the third category he included polygamy and the tribal custom of men and women sitting separately at public meetings. The categories are useful, but debate needs to continue on what customs should be included in which categories. Not all agreed with Bishop Gitari's list. In the West we do not see much polygamy, but we have many examples of living together without marriage and of what has been described as 'serial marriage'. What should be the attitude to this lifestyle when it comes to preparation for adult baptism and confirmation? What conditions, if any, should be set down?

How should the Decade affect leadership training?

This takes place in various categories. There is the training of laity in general. There is pre-ordination training in theological colleges and courses, followed by 'Post Ordination Training' and 'Continuing Ministerial Education'. There is also the training of Readers and of other 'Accredited Lay Ministries'.

Lambeth Resolution 44 suggests that there should be a greater mission dimension in all forms of training. How this can be done is one of the tasks of the Decade. It is partly a matter of understanding our modern secularised culture and knowing how to relate and communicate the gospel within it. It is a matter of learning the skills of 'recognising, co-ordinating and deploying'[45] the gifts and ministries of others. This is strategic to the task of mission and is partly a managerial task.

It is also a matter of recognising and using the style of leadership appropriate to each context and culture. In many urban cultures, for example, group leadership rather than solo leadership and decision by consensus rather than by voting is appropriate. The Liverpool diocese has set up a training course under the title 'Group for Urban Ministry and Leadership' (GUML) that takes groups of actual and potential leaders from certain urban parishes; it is considered essential that the incumbent is part of the group.

There are three questions that need to be asked –

1. What is the appropriate leadership which should be given by the ordained?
2. How should the ordained be engaging in shared leadership with the laity?
3. What form of lay leadership should be encouraged?

The above 'hard questions' are merely samples. There are many others. But the list will at least serve to illustrate the need for serious research and reflection. The Decade needs to be a time when we avoid both unreflective activism, but also 'analysis paralysis'.

Reflection needs to take place in the context of reaching out and making contact, and not be a substitute for it. Jack Burton is right to speak of the need for a sense of urgency. 'It is the urgency of knowing that lives are being lived at only half power: that vast areas of experience are being left undiscovered, undeveloped and unexplored; that talents are lying dormant; that love is being stunted and denied; that sin and selfishness are eating away at what, otherwise, would be lives of stature and achievement; that men and women are contenting themselves with husks, when they might be drinking of the water of life, freely'.[46]

Your Kingdom Come

The goal of the Decade is not simply to fill pews, but rather to pray that God's kingdom may come, that Christ's 'just and gentle rule' may be extended. This kingdom is not like an earthly, political kingdom, but nor is it purely 'spiritual'. Christ's rule is to be extended over every aspect of life. Some have used the idea of the kingdom in a mainly political sense and talked about it without reference to the Son of God. But you cannot be committed to the kingdom without being committed to the king. One description of Evangelism is therefore that of enlisting people for the reign of Christ.

The American writer, Jim Wallis, put it this way: 'Conversion is the beginning of active solidarity with the purposes of the kingdom of God..... We are converted to God and to God's purposes in history.... We are converted to compassion, justice and peace as we take our stand as citizens of Christ's new order'.[47]

To pray 'your kingdom come' is to pray, first, that Christ's reign may be extended over every part of our lives – including the library of our minds and the kitchen of our appetites. It is, also, to pray that every aspect of life in our congregation, our community, and our world may be brought under his rule. We pray this, not as a vain hope, but as a certainty that the day will come when Christ's rule is visibly and universally established, when the Father brings 'all things in heaven and on earth under one head, even Christ' (Ephesians 1.11). The world is not moving on to chaos; it is moving on to Christ.

QUESTIONS FOR DISCUSSION

Selection should be made from the following questions, according to need.

Evangelism and our faith journeys (see pages 3 to 11)

1. From the following definitions select those which you think are the most commonly used and those which you think are nearest to the truth –

    Getting people into church
    Making society more just
    Preaching Christianity
    Helping others
    Knocking on people's doors
    Announcing good news
    Making Christ known
    Holding open-air services
    Leading others to faith
    Organising a parish mission
    Making friends for Christ

What are the strengths and weaknesses of each one?
You may want to write your own definitions.

2. What have been the significant factors in your faith journey –
    parental influence
    the local church
    particular friends
    literature
    special mission events

How far has your faith journey been a process and how far a crisis?

3. Why are we often hesitant to share our faith?
    What help do we need?

4. What are the reasons why others find it hard to come to faith?
    What are the common barriers to belief?

The Local Church (pages 12 to 16)
5. What would a newcomer to our church find difficult? What can be done about it?
6. What steps can be taken to encourage real and relevant prayer and worship?
7. How much do we know about the local community? Do we need an audit?
8. In many churches ninety per cent of the work is done by ten per cent of the congregation. Is this true of our church? If so how can leadership and responsibility be shared?

Church-centred plans (pages 17 to 21)
9. How do people come into contact with the church and its members? (e.g. baptisms, weddings, the playgroup). Are there ways that contacts can be improved and followed up?
10. Are there areas of the parish where there is little contact? What can be done about it?
11. What specific groups are catered for already? (e.g. children, young marrieds). What other groups need to be contacted?

World-centred plans (pages 22 to 24)
12. What contacts do members of our congregation have with the local community and the wider world?
13. How can they be better equipped and supported in relating their faith to work, leisure pursuits and community affairs?

The Deanery and Churches Together in .... (pages 25 to 32)
14. Are there areas in our district where there is little contact with any of the churches? Is there a need for some kind of audit?
15. Are any of the ideas on pages 25 to 32 being used in your district? Are there any of them that should be seriously considered?
16. Is there help that could be given to, or received from, the churches outside our district? Are there ways in which we could receive the insights of the world church?

The 'Hard Questions' (pages 33 to 41)
These questions could also be used as a basis for discussion.

APPENDIX

Evangelism Books and Resources

Information on books and resources can normally be obtained from Diocesan Missioners and through Diocesan Mission, Education and Training departments. There are also resource lists available through the Board of Mission, Church House, Great Smith Street, Westminster, SW1P 3NZ (Tel. 071-222 9011).

Details of courses available and addresses of resource agencies are liable to change, but every effort has been made to ensure accuracy at the time of publishing the information below.

Evangelism Resource Agencies

A list compiled by Captain David Sanderson (CA)

Listed below are some of the main agencies which provide support, resources and sometimes people who can help in evangelism. However, there are others which can be found in the UK Christian Handbook 1992/93 (MARC/EA/Bible Society 1991 £21.99).

Additional Curates Society (ACS) 264a Washwood Heath Rd, Birmingham B8 2XS (021 328 0749). 'Follow Me' catechumenate nurture group course and prayer material.

Anglican Renewal Ministries (ARM) 45 Friar Gate, Derby DE1 1DA (0332 200175). 'Saints Alive', 9 unit course for small groups with video and other back up material. Evangelism training course and resources for renewal.

Arthur Rank Centre National Agricultural Society, Stoneleigh, Kenilworth, Warwicks. Specialises in rural mission.

BCMS Crosslinks 251 Lewisham Way, London SE4 1XF (081 691 6111) Help and advice with mission in multi-faith areas.

Bible Reading Fellowship (BRF) Peter's Way, Sandy Lane West, Oxford OX4 5HG (0865 748227. Bible reading materials to help lead people into faith and encourage evangelism.

Bible Society (BFBS) Stonehill Green, Westlea, Swindon SN5 7DG (0793 513713). Scriptures for distribution, church growth, small group training courses and evangelism resources.

Board of Mission (formerly part of Board for Mission and Unity BMU) Church House, Gt Smith St, Westminster, London SW1P 3NZ (071-222

9011). Help and advice on Mission and Evangelism. The decade of evangelism advisory team is part of the Board of Mission.

British Church Growth Association (BCGA), 3a Newnham St. Bedford MK40 2JR (0234 327905). Occasional Conferences, quarterly magazine *Church Growth Digest*, resource people.

Catechumenate Network Canon P.Ball, 'Whittonedge', Whittonditch Rd, Ramsbury, Marlborough, Wilts SN8 2PX (0672 20259). Regular training conferences, magazine and resource people.

Christian Enquiry Agency Inter-Church House 35 Lower Marsh, London SE1 7RL (071 620 4444) Country-wide network of follow up people for enquirers.

Christian Publicity Organisation (CPO) Garcia Estate, CanterburyRd, Worthing, West Sussex BN13 1BW (0903 64556). Extensive range of publicity and gospel leaflets. Materials for discipleship training, small groups and Bible study. Brochure available.

Christians in Sport P.O. Box 93, Oxford OX2 7YP (0865 311211). Evangelism through sport. Witness to the sporting community.

C.S. Lewis Centre 47 Bedford Square, London WC1B 3DP. Encourages a thoughtful approach to evangelism in the modern secular world.

Church Army Independents Rd, Blackheath, London SE3 9LG (081-318 1226) Evangelistic Training aids, training in evangelism and small group leadership. Mission teams available. Faith 4 2000 evangelism and training project.

Church Missionary Society (CMS), United Society for the Propagation of the Gospel (USPG), both at Partnership House, 175 Waterloo Rd, London SE1 8UU (071-928 8681). Help and materials on mission and evangelism in inter-faith situations.

Church's Ministry among Jews (CMJ) 30c Clarence Rd, St Albans AL1 4JJ (0727 833114). Expertise in ministry to the Jewish community.

Church Pastoral Aid Society (CPAS) Athena Drive, Tachbrook Park, Warwick CV34 6NG (0926 334242). Evangelism training, house group resources, materials for use in connection with occasional offices. Youth and Children's departments.

Church Planting in C of E Network co-ordinator Rev B Hopkins, 38 Lascells St, St Helen's, Merseyside WA9 1BA (0744 58886). Conferences, training days and other expertise

Church Union Renewal and Mission Committee Faith House, 7 Tufton St, London SW1P 3QN (071-222 6952). Prayer material and occasional leaflets.

Cliff College Calver, via Sheffield, Derbys S30 1XG (02458 2321). Methodist college offering a variety of evangelism training programmes.

Community of the Resurrection Mirfield WF14 0BN (0924 494318). Assistance for Parish missions, weekends, etc.

Council of Churches for Britain and Ireland (CCBI) Inter-church House 35 Lower Marsh, London SE1 7RL (071 620 4444) have evangelism resources especially relating to ecumenical activity. Material from the World Council of Churches (WCC) and the former British Council of Churches (BCC) is available from this address.

Department of Pastoral Formation, Archdiocese of Liverpool, 152 Brownlow Hill, Liverpool L3 5RQ 052. Useful workbook *Ministers of the Gospel* exploring the insights of Papal statements *Evangelii Nuntiandi* and *Redemptoris Missio*.

Deo Gloria Trust Selsdon House 212/220 Addington Rd, South Croydon, Surrey CR2 8LD (081 651 6428). Follow up network for enquirers. Help with the cults and occult.

Evangelical Coalition for Urban Mission (ECUM) Greg Smith, Lawrence Hall, Cumberland Rd, London E13 8NH (071-476 3651). Umbrella organisation drawing together evangelical groups concerned with inner cities. Expertise with Urban Mission.

Evangelical Alliance (EA) Whitefield House, 186 Kennington Park Rd, London SE11 4BT (071-582 0228). Various evangelism resources, consultation and training days.

Evangelism Explosion 228 Shirley Rd, Southampton SO1 3HR (0703 228985). Training courses for visitation evangelism.

Federation for Rural Evangelism Barry Osborne, 8 White Rock Rd, Hastings E. Sussex TN34 1LE (0424 712838). Ecumenical federation of groups and people involved in rural evangelism. Various resources.

Fellowship for Parish Evangelism Gavin Reid 138 St John's Rd. Woking, Surrey GU21 1PS (0483 715589). Missioners available for help with parish missions, etc.

The Gospel and Our Culture c/o Selly Oak Colleges, Bristol Rd, Selly Oak, Birmingham B29 6LQ. Exploration into the presentation of the Gospel in modern western society. Broadsheet and occasional conferences.

Home Evangelism (formerly Christian Colportage Association) (CCA) 3 Grange Rd, Egham Surrey TW0 9QW (0784 432558). Expertise with home visiting and residential conferences.

Office of Evangelisation 120 West Heath St, London NW3 7YT. Various R.C. evangelisation resources available for training in evangelism. Resource list available on request.

MARC Europe Vision Building, 4 Footscray Rd, Eltham, London SE9 2TZ (081-294 1989) Training Courses, statistical information, surveys. Brochure available.

Mothers' Union (MU) Mary Sumner House, 24 Tufton St, London SW1P 3RB (071 222 5533). Evangelism training course, material for evangelism among families, follow up on baptism, work with mums and toddlers.

The National Retreat Association, Liddon House, 24 South Audley St, London W1Y 5D1 (071-493 3534) provides information on all aspects of retreats and spiritual direction.

The Network Trust 100 Lazy Hill Rd, Aldridge, Walsall, West Midlands WS9 8RR (0922 52830) exists to promote evangelism through small groups as put forward in 'Good News Down Your Street'. Training weekends and visits to parishes.

One Step Forward Ministries 7 Purbeck Close, Long Eaton, Nottingham NG10 4PF (0602 734474). Evangelism training material and courses. Also offers a D.I.Y. continuing integrated programme of evangelism.

Open Air Campaigners 27, Adelaide Rd, Chichester, West Sussex PO19 4NB (0243 776914). Expertise and personnel available for a variety of outdoor evangelism.

Oxford Centre for Mission Studies Rev C. Sugden, St Philip and St James church, P.O. Box 70, Woodstock Rd, Oxford OX2 6MB (0865 56071). Courses on Mission and Culture, etc.

Rural Sunrise P.O. Box 14, Hastings, E. Sussex TN34 1BS (0424 712838). Evangelism and missions in rural areas.

Scripture Gift Mission (SGM) Radstock House, 3 Eccleston Street, London SW1W 9LZ (071 730 2155). Scriptures for distribution.

Scripture Union (SU) 130 City Rd, London EC1V 2NJ (071-782 0013). Training Unit at 26-30 Heathcoat St, Nottingham NG1 3AA. Leadership and House Group training, Bible study, house group and children's material.

S.E.A.N. The Pound, Whitestone, Exeter, Devon EX4 2HP (06476 1134) 'Abundant Life' — three bible study courses on the meaning of the Christian life. Have been successfully used in council house, inner city areas. Originally produced through the work of The South American Missionary Society.

Society of St Francis (Franciscans) House of Compassion, 42 Balaam St, London E13 8AQ. Prayer and parish missions, etc.

Urban Theology Unit 210 Abbeyfield Rd, Sheffield S4 7AZ (0742 435342). Training resource including library and courses for clergy and lay people in urban mission.

Youth for Christ (BYFC) Cleobury Place, Cleobury Mortimer, Kidderminster, Worcester DY14 8JG (0299 270260) Youth evangelism and training resources.

Mission Audit Resources

An Audit for the Local Church (BMU) £1. (£1.60 by post) obtainable through the Board of Mission

Mission Pursuit. URC Supplies, 86 Tavistock Place London WC1 9RT.

The Well Church Book John Finney, Scripture Union and CPAS. 1991. £5.95.

Books Quoted in the Text

Books for which prices are shown were in print at the time of going to press. Generally speaking these may be obtained through any bookseller (including Church House Bookshop, 31 Great Smith Street, London, SW1P 3BN: Tel. 071-222 5520). When titles are available from a single source of supply this is indicated. Publications of the Advisory Board of Ministry and of the Board of Mission may be obtained from Church House Bookshop.

All Are Called. CIO. 1985.

ACCM Occasional Paper No.22. 1987. £1. Obtainable from The Advisory Board of Ministry, Church House, Great Smith Street, SW1P 3NZ.

All God's Children? Nat.Society/CHP. 1991. £5.95.

The Call To Conversion. J.Wallis. Lion. 1984.

Christian Mission in the Modern World. J.R.W. Stott. Falcon. 1975 (Kingsway 1986).

The Church in the Market Place. G. Carey. Kingsway. 1984. £3.99.

The Church and Christian Union. S. Neill. OUP. 1968.

Creating Confidence in Evangelism. J.Young. CPAS. 1991. £3.95.

Evangelism in the Countryside. Board of Mission* 1991. £1 (by post £1.50).

Evangelism in the Early Church. M.Green. Highland. 1984. £4.50.

Everything's Possible. Methodist Publishing House.

From Everywhere to Everywhere. M. Nazir-Ali. Collins. 1991. £8.95.

The Gap. J.Burton. SPCK, 1991. £4.99.

God's Frozen People. M. Gibbs and R. Norton. Fontana. 1964.

Good News Down the Street. M.Wooderson. Grove Books. 1989. £1.60.

Good News in Our Times. The Gospel and Contemporary Cultures. CHP. 1991. £5.50. (Guide to study, *Gospel and Culture.* £1.50*.)

The Gospel and Contemporary Culture. H.Montefiore (Ed.) Mowbray 1992 £11.95.

The Gospel in a Pluralist Society. L. Newbigin. SPCK. 1989. £9.99.

Image Old and New. M. Ramsey. SPCK. 1963.

The Isaiah Vision. (An Ecumenical Strategy for Congregational Evangelism) R.Fung. WCC. 1992. £2.95.

Leadership Explosion. P. King. Hodder. 1987. £2.25. *

The Logic of Evangelism. W. Abraham. Hodder. 1989. £7.99.

Launch into the Decade. Southwell Diocese. 1990.

The Measure of Mission. CHP. 1987. £1.75.

The Missionary Shape of the Congregation. David Bridge. Methodist Publishing House.

Planting New Churches. G. Carey & others. Eagle 1991. £5.99.

Prayers for a Decade. CHP. £1.00.

The Truth Shall Make You Free. (1988 Lambeth Conference report) CHP. 1988. £8.50.

Twenty Things to do in a Decade of Evangelism. * 20p. £7 for 50.

Understanding Leadership. John Finney. Daybreak. 1989. £6.95.

The Well Church Book. John Finney. CPAS & Scripture Union. 1991. £5.95.

---

* Obtainable from the Board of Mission, Church House, Great Smith Street, London SW1P 3NZ (Tel. 071-222 9011)

NOTES

1. *Creating Confidence in Evangelism*, p.5.
2. *The Measure of Mission*, p.38.
3. *The Measure of Mission*, p.45.
4. *The Church and Christian Union*, p.75.
5. Details and comments on many of these statistics can be found in *All God's Children?* p.3 ff.
6. Lambeth Resolution 44; *The Truth Shall Make You Free*, p.231.
7. From a speech to The General Synod of the Church of England by Archbishop Lord Runcie; November 1990.
8. From *Launch into the Decade*; Southwell Diocese, June 1990.
9. *Christian Mission in the Modern World*, p.81.
10. *Image Old and New*, p.14.
11. *Theology*, Nov.-Dec. 1991, p.405.
12. *Good News in Our Times*, p.26.
13. *The Logic of Evangelism*, p.95.
14. From an address at a Swanwick Conference, 1974.
15. *The Truth Shall Make You Free*, p.231.
16. See page 29 below.
17. Quoted in *Prayers for a Decade*, p. 7.
18. *Evangelism in the Countryside*, p. 19.
19. A Methodist publication *Everything's Possible* gives descriptions of a number of churches transformed with a little imagination and expertise.
20. For details see list of books used in text.
21. Available from The Rev. Lindsay Urwin, 1 New Dorset Street, Brighton BN1 3LL.
22. *From Everywhere to Everywhere*, p. 140.
23. *Evangelism in the Countryside*, p. 10.
24. Details from The Evangelical Alliance. Whitfield House, 186 Kennington Park Road, London, SE11 4BT.
25. *The Missionary Shape of the Congregation*.

26. Ideas on vision, goal setting and delegation can be found in *Leadership Explosion*, *Understanding Leadership*, and in publications from MARC Europe.
27. ACCM Occasional Paper 22, p.29.
28. *Good News in our Times*, p. 88.
29. *All are Called*, p. 39.
30. *The Gap*, p.46.
31. *God's Frozen People*, p.111.
32. *The Gospel in a Pluralist Society*, p.238.
33. Information on Local Ecumenical Projects (LEPs) can be obtained from the Council for Christian Unity, Church House, Great Smith Street, Westminster.
34. Two organisations in this area are Careforce (130 City Road, London EC1V 2NJ) and Time for God (2 Chester House, Pages Lane, London N10 1PR).
35. Names and addresses of secretaries can be obtained from Churches Together in England, Inter-Church House, 35-41 Lower Marsh, London SE1 7RL.
36. *The Truth Shall Make You Free*, p.32.
37. Much of the material in this section can be found in fuller form in the chapter by the Rev.Eric Shegog in *Opportunities and Limitations in Religious Broadcasting* edited by Peter Elvy. Edinburgh University Press. Obtainable from The Centre for Theology and Press Issues, New College, Edinburgh.
38. *The Isaiah Vision*, p.29.
39. *The Truth Shall Make You Free*, p.34.
40. *Good News in Our Times*, p.34f.
41. *Evangelism in the Early Church*, p.83.
42. *Good News in our Times*, pp.18-19.
43. *Evangelism in the Early Church*, p.73.
44. p.42.
45. ACCM Occasional Paper 22, p.29.
46. *The Gap*, p.37.
47. *The Call to Conversion*, pp. 5, 7, 9.